CONTENTS

DO YOU BELIEVE IN MAGIC?

If you do, you probably *won't* make a very good magician! You see, good magicians know there's really no such thing as magic. Magicians are masters of *illusion*. They can make things look like something they're not. Magic tricks take quick hands, fast talk, and good showmanship! *And* magic tricks take practice.

Many of the tricks in this book depend on *sleight of hand.* That means your hands move faster than the eyes of the people watching you. Stand in front of a mirror as you practice each trick. When your hands move so quickly that you almost fool yourself, you're ready to perform in front of friends.

Practice your *patter*, or "fast, silly talk." Magicians use patter to make the audience think about what they're saying instead of what they're doing. Make your patter as funny as you can. Fumble your words. Tell silly jokes. If you make a mistake, turn it into a joke—make it part of your patter.

MORE MAGIC TRICKS
YOU CAN DO

Written by Judith Conaway
Illustrated by Renzo Barto

Troll Associates

Library of Congress Cataloging in Publication Data

Conaway, Judith (date)
    More magic tricks you can do.

    Summary: Provides instructions for sixteen simple
magic tricks using matchboxes, marbles, scarves, coins,
rope, and other items. Includes tips on practicing,
choosing a costume and a name, and performing.
    1. Tricks—Juvenile literature.   [1. Magic tricks]
I. Barto, Renzo, ill.   II. Title.
GV1548.C66   1987   793.8   86-11351
ISBN 0-8167-0864-9 (lib. bdg.)
ISBN 0-8167-0865-7 (pbk.)

Say something like this: "Oh, no! Ladies and gentlemen, the forces of evil are at work in this room, trying to break my magic spells. Begone, evil spirits! Try *this* one on for size!" Then move quickly on to your next trick.

Your costume is another important part of the show. Wearing a magician's costume will add to the fun! Many magicians wear black suits and top hats. Others wear gypsy fortune-teller's costumes or dress to look like circus performers. Choose the costume that is most comfortable for you.

Then give yourself a name. Here are a few suggestions:

> *Mondo the Magnificent*
> *Houdini Hal*
> *Abra K. Dabra*
> *The Incredible Illusionist*
> *The Wizard of* (name of
> your town)

Once you have chosen your name, make posters to advertise your show. Then use the magic tricks in this book to delight and surprise your friends. And, most of all, have fun!

MATCHBOX MIX

Red paper in one box
And blue in another—
Till magically switched
From one to the other.

Here's what you need:

Red and blue crayons

Scissors

2 Identical,
empty matchboxes

Ruler

Red and blue
construction paper

Here's what you do to prepare:

1 Cut two 1½-inch squares from construction paper: one red and one blue.

2 Draw a red dot on the end of one matchbox drawer and a blue dot on the end of the other, as shown. Practice sliding the drawers halfway open, so that the dots are hidden beneath the box covers.

Here's how to perform the trick:

1 Show the audience the two small squares of paper. Then show the empty matchboxes. Remember to keep the secret dots hidden when you open the drawers!

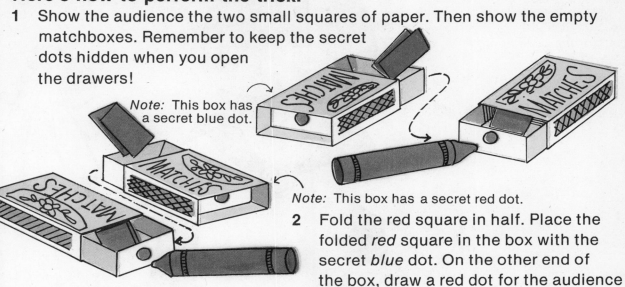

Note: This box has a secret blue dot.

Note: This box has a secret red dot.

2 Fold the red square in half. Place the folded *red* square in the box with the secret *blue* dot. On the other end of the box, draw a red dot for the audience to see.

3 Fold the blue square in half. Place the folded *blue* square in the box with the secret *red* dot. On the other end of the box, draw a *blue* dot for the audience to see.

4 Pick up the boxes. Place them one on top of the other, and hold them over your head. Say some magic words, ending with the command, "Pass!" As you bring the boxes back down turn them so that the secret dots face the audience.

5 Now open the boxes. The colored squares will appear to have switched places!

LOSE YOUR MARBLES

Marble, marble
In a hanky.
Shake it—
Now it's hanky-panky!

Here's what you need:

1 Small
rubber band

2 Identical
marbles

1 Small box with removable lid

1 Handkerchief

Tape

Here's what you do to prepare:

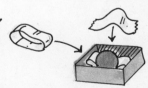

1   Remove the box lid. Cut a small piece of tape and fashion it into a circle, with the sticky side facing out. Press the circle of tape flat against the box lid.

2   Press one of the marbles firmly onto the tape. Put another piece of tape over the marble, attaching it to the lid. Place the box lid gently back on the box.

3   Put a small rubber band around the first joint of your left middle finger and ring finger, as shown.

Here's how to perform the trick:

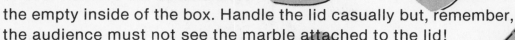

1 Hold up the box for your audience to see. Remove the lid and show the empty inside of the box. Handle the lid casually but, remember, the audience must not see the marble attached to the lid!

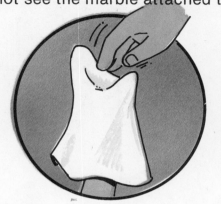

2 Take the other marble out of your pocket and give it to a member of the audience. Spread the handkerchief over your left hand while attention is on the audience member.

3 Beneath the handkerchief, slide your thumb into the rubber band and stretch the band open. With your right hand, make an indent in the top of the handkerchief. Ask the person to drop the marble into the well.

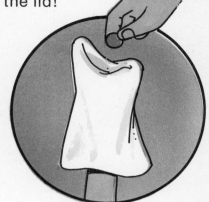

4 Now slide the rubber band off your fingers and thumb. It will wrap around the marble as shown. As the rubber band slides off, take one corner of the handkerchief in your right hand. Shake it! It will look like the marble has vanished!

5 Now pick up the box and shake it hard. The marble will come loose and start to rattle. Open the box and let the marble roll out. Your audience will be amazed!

SCARVES FROM THIN AIR

Inside and out
There's nothing about
Till magic is there
To make scarves from thin air!

Here's what you need:

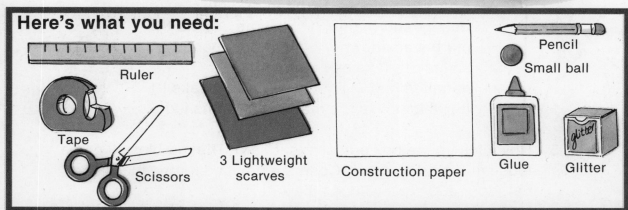

Ruler

Tape

Scissors

3 Lightweight scarves

Construction paper

Pencil

Small ball

Glue

Glitter

Here's what you do to prepare:

1 To make a tube for your secret compartment, roll a sheet of construction paper into a cylinder and tape it together as shown.

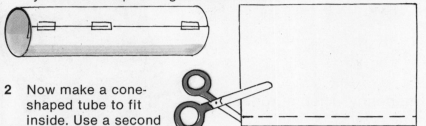

2 Now make a cone-shaped tube to fit inside. Use a second sheet of construction paper. (Be sure it is the same size and color as the first.) Trim off ¼ inch along one of the long sides. Then cut along both short sides of the paper from the bottom corners to one inch in at the top. Roll the paper into a cone shape and tape it together as shown.

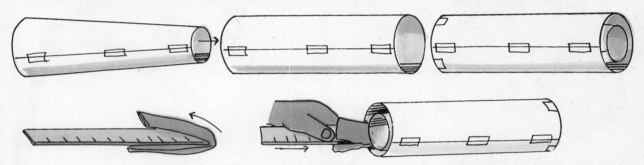

3 Fit the cone inside the cylinder. Tape the tubes together at the end where the openings are the same size. If you like, decorate your "magic" tube with glitter.

4 Fold a scarf into a long narrow strip. Set a ruler on top of half the scarf. Fold the other half over the ruler. Use the ruler to stuff the scarf into the space between the two tubes. Insert the other scarves in the same way. Be sure the scarves are completely hidden from your audience.

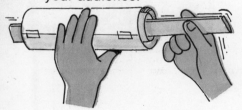

Here's how to perform the trick:

1 Show the tube to your audience, but be sure to only let them see the end where the two tubes join. Pass a ruler through the tube or drop a ball through the tube to "prove" that the tube is "hollow."

2 Now wave your hand in front of the tube and say some magic words. Pull out the scarves, one-by-one, and watch the surprise on the faces in your audience!

THE GREAT COIN CAPER

Make it safe.
Fold up your penny.
But *oops!* Watch out!
There isn't any!

Have a volunteer provide the penny. Then surprise everyone with this trick!

Here's what you need:

Scissors

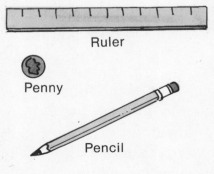

Ruler

Penny

Pencil

Paper

Here's what you do to prepare:

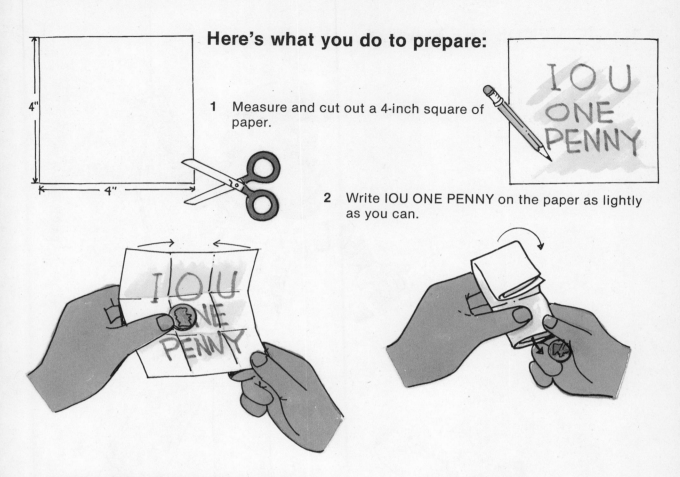

1 Measure and cut out a 4-inch square of paper.

2 Write IOU ONE PENNY on the paper as lightly as you can.

Here's how to perform the trick:

1 Hold the paper in your hand with the written side facing you. Place the penny in the center of the paper. Fold the bottom third up and the top third down to cover the penny.

2 Turn the paper slightly as shown. As you fold the top third down, let the penny drop out of the opening and into your hand. Don't let anyone see it fall!

3 Now fold the bottom third up. Give the packet to the person who gave you the penny. Ask that person to open the packet and show the audience the penny inside.

4 When the penny's owner unfolds the packet and finds no penny, ask him or her to read the message inside. When the laughter dies down, return the penny to its owner.

MAGIC MENDS THE ROPE

Snip, snip—
The rope's in two.
Until my magic
Works like glue!

Here's what you need:

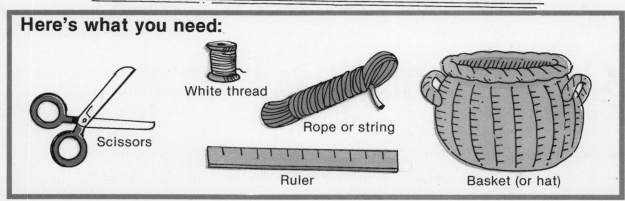

Scissors

White thread

Rope or string

Ruler

Basket (or hat)

Here's what you do to prepare:

1 Cut a 3-foot length of rope, a 6-inch length of rope, and a 4-inch length of white thread.

2 Bend the 6-inch length of rope into a loop. Wrap the thread around the ends of the loop. Tie a double knot.

3 Slip the 3-foot length of rope through the loop. Slide the loop to the middle of the rope.

Here's how to perform the trick:

1 Have a basket (or hat) and a pair of scissors on a table before you. Hold the rope with the loop in your hands as shown. (It will seem to the audience that the two separate lengths of rope are really one!)

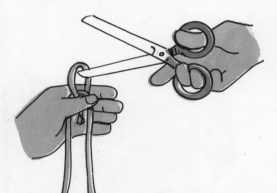

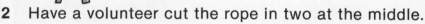

2 Have a volunteer cut the rope in two at the middle.

3 Place the middle of the rope into the basket, leaving the ends hanging over the sides. As you take your hands out of the basket, push the loop to the side so that it is not touching the rope.

4 Wave your hands mysteriously over the hat and say some magic words. Then slowly raise the rope out of the hat as shown. When the entire rope is visible, pull tightly on both ends to show that you have "magically" restored it to one long piece!

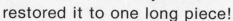

MAGIC-SCARF KNOT TRICK

With only one hand
A knot I'll twist,
With magical words
And a flick of the wrist!

Here's what you need:

Long scarf

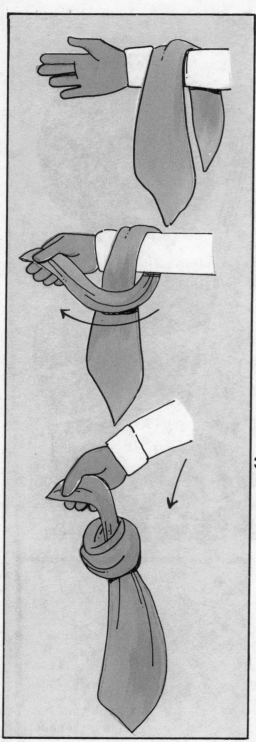

Here's how to perform the trick:

1 Present the scarf to the audience and drape it over your right arm. Be sure that the longer end of the scarf hangs over the left side of your arm. Announce that most people need two hands to tie a knot, but that you have a magic scarf that can be knotted by using only one hand!

2 With your left hand, loop the short end of the rope around your right wrist and over the long end of the rope as shown. Place the short end of the scarf in your right hand, keeping the loop as loose as possible. (If you do this while you introduce the trick, no one will notice that you used your left hand.)

3 With your right arm extended, say some magic words. Then flip the loop off your wrist by quickly flicking your arm toward the floor. Pull your hand through the loop, holding tightly onto the short end of the scarf. Now hold up the scarf for all to see—there will be a knot in it!

Practice this trick and it will become easy to perform. And it will look *magnificent!*

THE SHREDDED PAPER TRICK

Hot off the press
I'll rip and shred,
Till *abracadabra*
It can still be read!

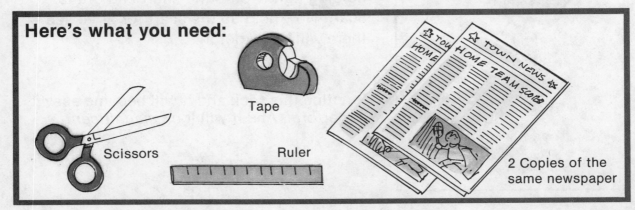

Here's what you need:

Tape

Scissors

Ruler

2 Copies of the same newspaper

Here's what you do to prepare:

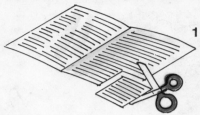

1 Separate the front page from each of two identical newspapers. Measure and cut out a 5-inch square from a left-over page. Tape the square to the inside corner of one of the front pages. Tape only three sides, leaving the top open to form a pocket.

2 Fold the front page without the pocket the long way. Fold it three times to form a narrow

strip. Then fold crosswise, twice. Press down so that the paper is very flat. Fit the folded page into the hidden pocket.

Here's how to perform the trick:

1 Hold up the front page with the hidden pocket as shown. The hidden pocket should be facing *you* and not your audience! Holding the corner with the pocket in your hand, tear the paper. Rip from top to bottom and then from side to side, forming pieces about the size of the hidden pocket.

2 As you tear the page, tear open the pocket. Slip the folded page out and hide it behind the pieces in your hand.

3 When you have finished tearing the newspaper, pass the torn pieces from hand to hand. Say some magic words. Then turn the pieces over in your hand so that the folded page is facing the audience and the torn pieces are behind it.

4 Open the folded page all the way out! Slip the torn pieces into your shirt, your pocket, or under your belt while you are hidden behind the paper. Now smooth out the paper with both hands.

Your audience will be amazed!

CARD COME UP!

You push the card,
It will not rise.
I push the card,
What a surprise!

Here's what you need:

Bar of soap

Empty glass

Playing card

Here's what you do to prepare:

On the inside of the glass, draw a thin line of soap. Draw another line of soap directly across from the first line.

Here's how to perform the trick:

1   Line the card up along the two lines of soap as shown. Then push the card down into the glass.

2   Immediately clap your hands and say some magic words. The card will rise up in the glass.

3   Now ask someone in the audience to come forward and try the trick. This time be sure to push the card down where it will not touch the lines of soap. The card will not rise.

That proves it—it's magic!

SUPER SALT TRICK

Tear a tissue.
Easy, right?
But with my salt
You'll try all night!

Here's what you need:

Tissues

Salt

Paper-towel tube

Broomstick

Rubber band

Here's how to perform the trick:

1 Have all your materials before you on a table. Hold up the tube to show the audience that it is hollow. Stretch a tissue across the opening of the tube and fasten it to the tube with a rubber band.

2 Ask the members of the audience if they think it would be easy to tear the tissue. Have a volunteer come forward and try to tear the tissue by pushing a broomstick through the tube. (Of course, the tissue will tear!)

3 Now bring out the salt. Tell the audience that you are going to cast a magic spell on the salt to make it stronger than anyone in the room. Say some magic words.

4 Stretch another piece of tissue over the tube and fasten it with a rubber band. This time pour three inches of salt into the tube. Have another volunteer try to tear the tissue. No one will be able to do it!

Here's how the trick *really* works:

There are thousands of tiny spaces between the crystals of salt. When the stick is pushed into the salt, the crystals bump against each other, and the force of the stick is pushed in a thousand different directions. So really, all the pressure you put on the stick is swallowed by the huge number of spaces between the salt crystals! But to someone watching—it's magic!

MORE SUPER SALT

Lift this ice with string, you say?
Super salt's the only way!

Here's what you need:

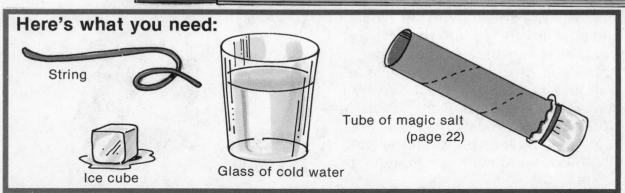

String

Ice cube

Glass of cold water

Tube of magic salt
(page 22)

Here's how to perform the trick:

1 Put an ice cube in a glass of cold water. Show the glass of water to the audience.

2 Now pull a piece of string from your pocket. The string should be about 6 inches long. Have several volunteers come forward and try, without tying any knots, to lift the ice above the glass, using only the 6-inch length of string.

3 When everyone is satisfied that this cannot be done, tell the audience they are right! The only way that the string can lift the ice cube is by the power of magic super salt!

4 Take out the tube of magic salt (see page 22) and say some magic words over it. Then sprinkle a line of salt over the top of the ice and string. (Be sure the middle of the string is lying over the middle of the ice cube.)

5 Now lift the string by the end, straight out of the glass. The ice cube will cling to it!

SHADOW PUPPETS

The lights! The magic! It's theater. Nothing is more fun than a play—and what a big change from paper and sticks to funny characters! On page 32, you'll find out how to make a stage for your puppets that seems to make them come alive.

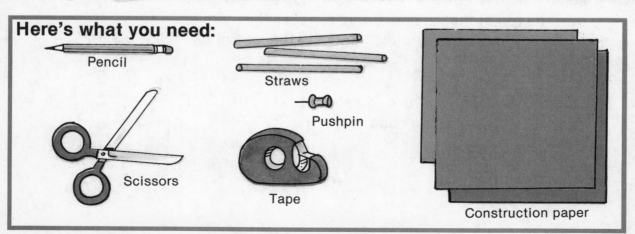

Here's what you need:

Pencil

Straws

Pushpin

Scissors

Tape

Construction paper

Here's what you do:

1 Think of what your play is going to be about. What characters would be fun—animals, people, make-believe creatures?

2 Draw puppet characters on construction paper. Remember that shadow puppets are seen as the outline you cut and the places you pierce on paper to let the light shine through. The shape should be simple, but distinctive enough to tell what the character is. The following pages show some shapes you can use. Or, if you like, make up some shapes of your own!

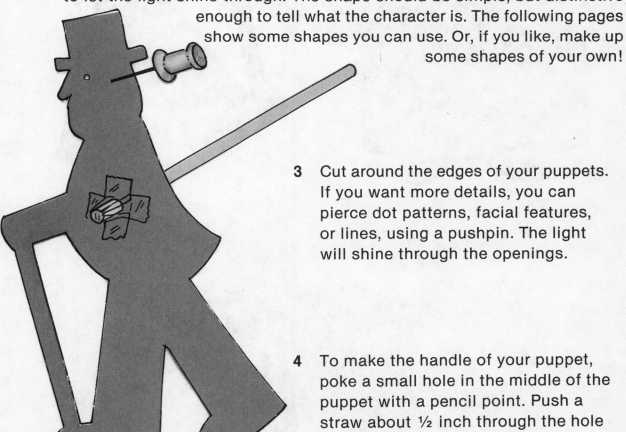

3 Cut around the edges of your puppets. If you want more details, you can pierce dot patterns, facial features, or lines, using a pushpin. The light will shine through the openings.

4 To make the handle of your puppet, poke a small hole in the middle of the puppet with a pencil point. Push a straw about ½ inch through the hole and tape it securely into place as shown.

SHADOW THEATER

Now that you have a cast of characters for your show,
you need a stage where they can perform.

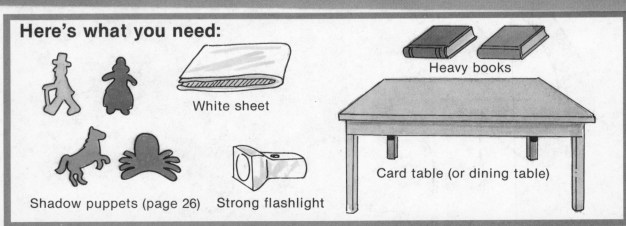

Here's what you need:

White sheet

Heavy books

Shadow puppets (page 26)   Strong flashlight

Card table (or dining table)

Here's what you do:

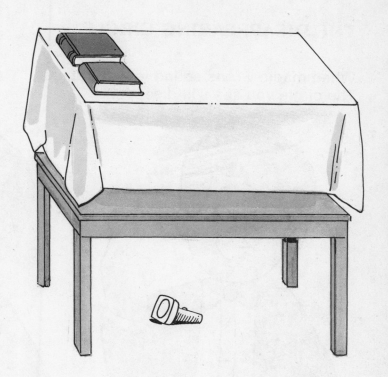

1   First, you must find a good place for your stage. A card table or dining table is a simple solution. Spread the sheet over the table. Secure the sheet by putting heavy books over it as shown. Place your flashlight behind the sheet. Turn off all the other lights to make the room as dark as possible.

2   When the puppets touch the back of the sheet, they show through to the audience as shadows. (*Note:* The rest of the "backstage" will not show through the sheet, unless it brushes up against the sheet itself. So be careful not to touch the sheet—or you'll be onstage, too!)

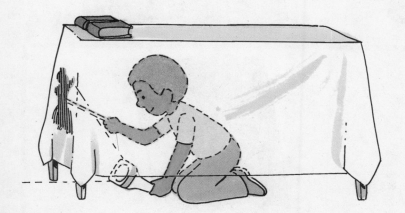

THE DISAPPEARING CIRCLE

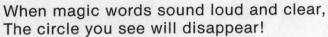

When magic words sound loud and clear,
The circle you see will disappear!

Here's what you need:

3 Rubber bands

Rubber or metal washer

Jacket

Here's what you do to prepare:

1   Fasten the washer to a rubber band by pushing one loop of the band through the washer. Pass the loop back through the other end of the band as shown. Then pull on the loop to tighten the knot.

2   Using the same method, attach the second rubber band to the first. Then attach the third rubber band to the second.

3   Slip the end rubber band around your wrist and over your elbow. Then put on your jacket. Stretch the rubber bands so that you can easily hold the washer between your thumb and forefinger. Be sure to keep the rubber bands hidden from your audience!

Here's how to perform the trick:

1   Show the ring to your audience and say, "Watch closely! You won't believe your eyes! I will magically make this ring disappear."

2   Say some magic words. Then toss the ring up into the air. The bands on your arm will pull the washer up into your sleeve. Open your hand to show the audience it is empty. They truly will not believe their eyes!

Practice this trick in front of a mirror. Make sure you always keep the back of your hand to the audience and the rubber bands hidden in your palm.

VEGETABLE VOODOO

Inside a bag
Lies a can of food.
I'll magically switch it
To suit my mood!

Here's what you need:

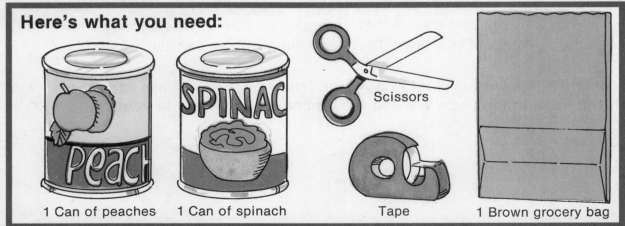

1 Can of peaches   1 Can of spinach   Scissors   1 Brown grocery bag

Here's what you do to prepare:

1 Remove the label from the can of spinach. To do this, run the point of a scissors' blade down the label along the seam. Then carefully peel the label off the can.

2 Put the label from the spinach around the can of peaches. Fasten the label with an inch-long piece of tape. Fold one end of the tape over itself to make a tab as shown.

Here's how to perform the trick:

1 Begin with the following story: *The other day my mother brought home a can of spinach from the supermarket.* Shake open the bag to show that it is empty.

2 Hold up the can with the phony spinach label. Place the can inside the bag and continue: *When she told me what was in the bag, I cringed. I decided only vegetable voodoo could save the day! I closed my eyes.* (Close your eyes.) *I put my hands on top of my head.* (Put your hands on top of your head.) *And I said, "Vegetable, my mood to suit— change yourself into a fruit!"*

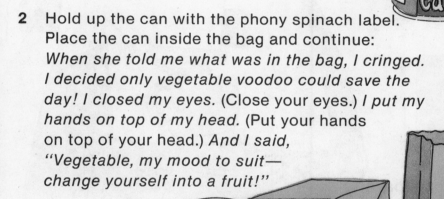

3 Reach into the bag and quickly pull off the phony label, using the tab. Leave the label in the bag. (Be sure it remains hidden from the audience.) Take out the can of peaches!

4 Say something to close the trick. For example, *Now I just have to learn how to turn a grocery bag into a can opener!*

SAWING A SNAKE IN HALF

A snake in an envelope
Means magic and fun.
You cut it in two—
But it comes out as one!

Here's what you need:

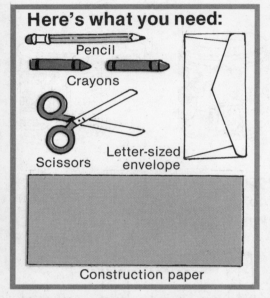

Pencil

Crayons

Scissors

Letter-sized
envelope

Construction paper

Here's what you do to prepare:

1 Use this pattern to make a snake out of construction paper. Fold the construction paper in half. Open, and color the snake. Now make another snake exactly like the first one.

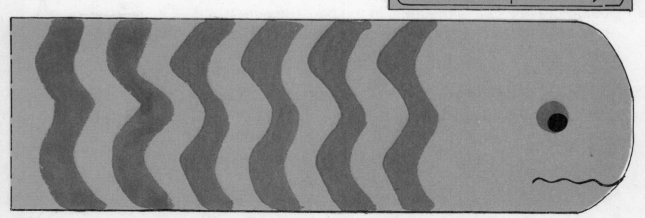

2 Make a slit on the ends of the envelope as shown. The slits should be wide enough for the snake to pass through easily.

Here's how to perform the trick:

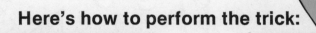
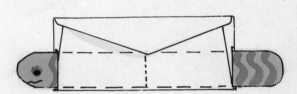

1 Fold one of the snakes in half. Hold the two snakes together so that the folded snake is hidden behind the other.

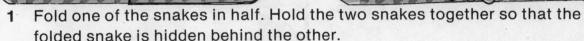

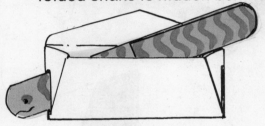

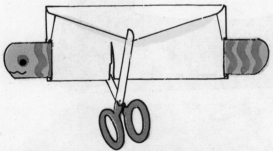

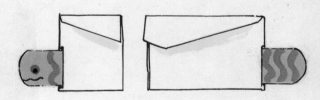

2 Announce that you are going to cut the snake in half and then put it back together by magic. Hold the envelope in front of you. Say some magic words. Then insert the snakes as shown.

3 Using a pair of scissors, cut the envelope in half.

4 Be sure to cut toward the head of the unfolded snake, so that you don't cut the snake that is folded. Hold the two halves of the envelope apart for your audience to see.

THE MYSTERIOUS MESSAGE

The envelope's empty—
Nothing's inside.
But a message appears
When you open it wide!

Here's what you need:

Pencil

Glue

Scissors

White paper

2 Identical envelopes

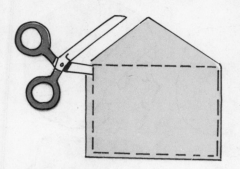 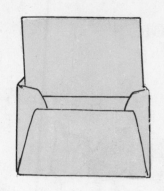 

Here's what you do to prepare:

1   Cut out the front side of an envelope as shown. Open the second envelope. Slide the piece you just cut into the second envelope to be sure it fits. Cut a small piece of white paper. Write the answer to a question you plan to ask the audience on the white paper.

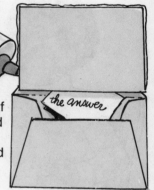

2   Slide the loose piece of paper out of the envelope. Apply a thin line of glue along three edges where shown. (*Note:* The glue should be applied to the *back* of the paper.) Place the answer in the envelope. Then carefully slide in the glued piece of paper, so that the answer is trapped between the envelope and the glued sheet.

Here's how to perform the trick:

1   Tell your audience that you are going to get a message from the spirits. The message will appear inside an empty envelope. Open the envelope to show it's really empty.

2   Now tell the audience the question you are going to ask the spirits. Write it on a piece of paper and put it inside the envelope. Seal the envelope and place it on the floor in front of you.

3   Give the audience your best magician's patter. You may even want to do a few dance steps around the envelope to conjure up the spirits!

4   Open the envelope by tearing off one end. Reach inside the secret pocket, take out the answer slip, and read your message from the spirits aloud. Your audience will be amazed!

COMMAND OF COLOR

Balls of color
In a sack.
Pick one out—
I'll give it back!

Here's what you need:

2 Quart-size plastic bags

4 Different colors of tissue paper

Scissors

Double-faced tape

Here's what you do to prepare:

1 Cut 3 colors of tissue paper into 2-inch squares. Cut 10 squares of each color. Cut the fourth color (let's say red) into 25 squares. Crumple the squares into balls.

2 Lay one plastic bag flat on a table. Run a strip of double-faced tape along each side of the bag as shown. Line up the second bag on top of the first, so that the open ends of both bags are on the same side. Press the second bag firmly to the taped areas. You now have one bag with two separate compartments.

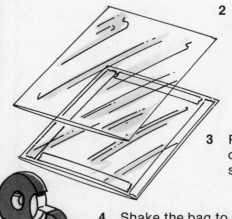

3 Put 15 red tissue balls in one side of the bag. Put all the other balls (including the 10 remaining red balls) into the other side of the bag.

4 Shake the bag to mix the colors. Roll down the top inch-and-a-half of the plastic bag, so that the side with the 15 red balls is closed and only the side with the 40 mixed balls can be touched.

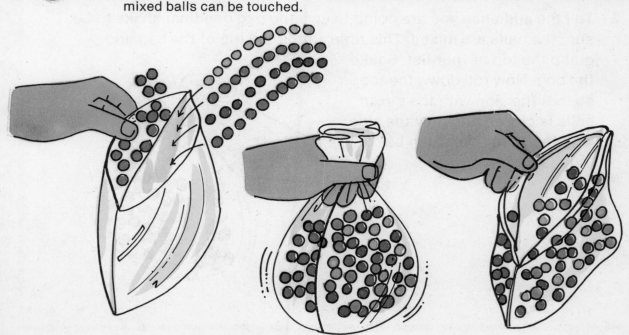

Here's how to perform the trick:

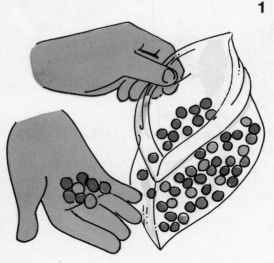

1 Show the bag to your audience. Shake the bag. Take out a handful of balls and point out the different colors. Put the balls back in the bag.

2 Tell the audience you are going to give the bag one final shake to be sure the balls are mixed. This time, unroll the top of the bag and grasp the top in your fist. Shake the bag. Now roll down the top, so that the side with the mixed balls is closed and only the side with the 15 red balls can be touched.

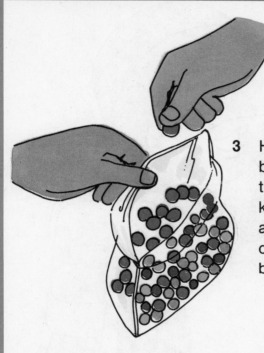

3 Have a volunteer come forward and pick a ball from the bag. Turn your back and hold the bag out behind you. (Be sure to always keep the side with the mixed balls toward the audience.) Tell the volunteer to look at the color and concentrate hard, but to keep the ball hidden in his or her fist.

4 Now turn to your audience. Explain that you will attempt to pick out the same color ball as now lies in the volunteer's fist. Ask for quiet and pretend you are concentrating. Turn your back again. Slowly reach into the bag and pick out a ball. Hold up the ball as you place the bag out of the way. Turn around and ask the volunteer to reveal the colors. Of course, both balls will be red!

As the audience applauds, ask your volunteer to take a bow, saying that this person's mind was unusually easy to read!

NUMERICALLY THINKING

Any number
You can name—
I shall guess
The very same!

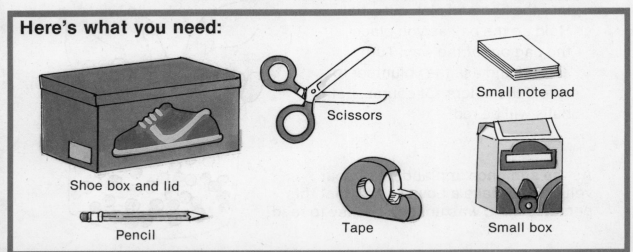

Here's what you need:

Shoe box and lid

Pencil

Scissors

Tape

Small note pad

Small box

Here's what you do to prepare:

1 Use scissors to cut a slit about 2 inches long into the bottom of the shoe box. Attach a small open-topped box inside the shoe box with tape. The open side of the small box should be directly beneath the slit.

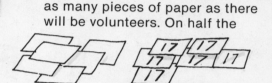

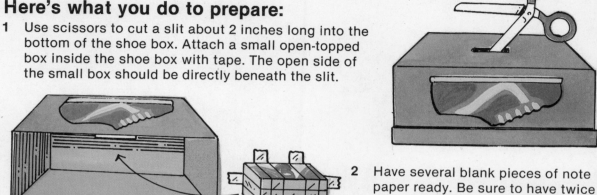

2 Have several blank pieces of note paper ready. Be sure to have twice as many pieces of paper as there will be volunteers. On half the pieces of paper write the number 17. Fold each one and put them in the open lid of the shoe box. Then put the shoe box over the lid.

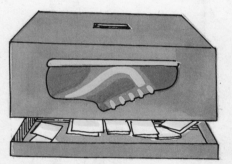

Here's how to perform the trick:

1 Ask each of your volunteers to secretly write any number from 1 to 20 on a slip of paper. Have them fold the paper and put it into the box through the slit.

2 Shake the box and then remove the top. With your eyes closed, pick one of the slips in the lid and hand it to a volunteer. Have that person look at the number. After you have meditated for a short time, announce that the number on the slit is 17.

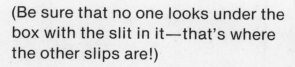

(Be sure that no one looks under the box with the slit in it—that's where the other slips are!)